Schumacher College Paper No. 1

Economic Renaissance

Holistic Economics for the 21st Century

SCHUMACHER COLLEGE Paper No. 1

Economic Renaissance

Holistic Economics for the 21st Century

Colin Tudge
Introduction by Satish Kumar

Dartington

An informal account by Colin Tudge of a think-tank held at SCHUMACHER COLLEGE, Devon in November 2007, on *Holistic Economics*

First published in 2008
by Schumacher College
as an initiative of The Dartington Hall Trust

Schumacher College
The Old Postern,
Dartington, Totnes TQ9 6EA
www.schumachercollege.org.uk

Distributed by Green Books Ltd
Foxhole, Dartington, Totnes,
Devon TQ9 6EB
www.greenbooks.co.uk

The Dartington Hall Trust is a company limited by guarantee, registered in England as a charity. *Company no. 1485560, charity no. 279756, VAT no. 402196875. Registered office: The Elmhirst Centre, Dartington Hall, Totnes, Devon TQ9 6EL.*

Printed by ImprintDigital

Text printed on Corona Natural (100% recycled)

A catalogue record for this publication
is available from the British Library

ISBN 978 1 900322 34 8

Contents

Introduction

by Satish Kumar

There is a big problem with the economy, namely that it is disconnected from both ecology and equity. In the past hundred years the economy has grown twenty-fold, yet during the same period the ecological capital of the Earth and the livelihoods of hundreds of millions of people have been in constant decline.

In spite of the many efforts and good intentions of governments, UN agencies and NGOs, the Earth's natural resources have continued to be pillaged. Economic growth has been matched only by the growth of the gap between rich and poor. Moreover, nobody seems to know how to address this fundamental fault line in the economy.

In the light of this predicament, in November 2007 Schumacher College organised a think tank bringing together a group of holistic economists who share a vision of a new economic order which can simultaneously bring about ecological sustainability and human wellbeing. The group spent three days at the College exploring practical ways and means of economic transformation and developing a cohesive framework for a new economic order based on the principles of equity, sustainability and spirituality. They addressed the following questions:

What are the key components of an economic system which would successfully achieve poverty elimination, climate sustainability and human fulfilment?

How can we bring about systemic change to address the root causes of the present economic crisis rather than treat the symptoms?

What kind of economy do we need to protect ecosystems and people's livelihoods at the same time?

After three days of extensive discussions and deliberations we agreed that an economic "renaissance" is needed to meet the enormous challenges of sustainability, equity and climate change. In particular, we need to redesign our food systems, energy systems and money systems in order to create a new economic order. Food, energy and money are the three fundamental components which need root and branch reform.

Colin Tudge, who participated in the discourse throughout, was given the task of summarising the essential spirit and pertinent points of the discussions held. This small book is the result. Colin has been able to capture the intricate arguments of the participants in a most admirable and impressive way. There is a wonderful combination of idealism and pragmatism in this book. I hope that economists, environmentalists, politicians and business leaders will find here a direction which has wisdom and vision as well as enough material for practical action.

At the end of the three days we agreed to establish two working groups: one called Polestars and the other Flashpoints.

The responsibility of the Polestars is to develop the big picture and create a new vision, new analysis and new theories of holistic economics on a long-term basis; whereas Flashpoints will focus on action and implementation, responding to the day-to-day events impacting on ecology and equity.

It was agreed that the second think tank will take place in November 2008.

Last but not least, I would like to express my sincere thanks to Cherian Eapen for his generous support, financial contribution and participation in the discourse. Without his sponsorship this gathering would not have been possible.

Also, I would like to thank James Martin-Jones who facilitated the think tank in a most efficient and coherent manner. Without his diligent and focused facilitation we would not have been able to achieve such a remarkable outcome.

Chapter 1

What's the Problem?

We, human beings, at least in our recognizably modern form, are a new species. Biologically speaking, we should be at the beginning of our run. There seems to be no fundamental reason to doubt that our descendants could still be here in a million years. We should be thinking seriously about the next 10,000 years. One thousand years should be a standard unit of political time.

Instead, we seem to be staring Armageddon in the face. Sober commentators including Britain's Archbishop of Canterbury and the President of the Royal Society have predicted of late that we will be lucky to survive the 21st century in a recognizable and tolerable form.

Already, according to the United Nations, out of a world population of around 6.5 billion, about one billion are chronically undernourished – while another one billion eat too much, and are dying from diabetes and heart disease. Privation cannot be assessed simply in cash terms, but in a world that is increasingly dominated by money, cash clearly matters: and the register tells us that in a world awash with multi-millionaires, one billion contrive to live on less than a dollar a day, while almost half of us live on less than two dollars a day. An estimated one billion live in urban slums. Much lip service is paid to the ideas of justice and democracy yet year by year, inexorably and demonstrably, the rich grow richer and the poor grow poorer. We still speak of war "breaking out" as if peace was the norm but in truth, most of the major countries have been waging war more often than not, somewhere or other, over the past several centuries. For most of the world, war rather than peace is the default position. At the same time our fellow creatures are in the throes of the most rapid mass extinction the world has ever seen, and one of the most extensive; vital resources are fast running out; and — seemingly the coup de grace — the world is warming up. Global warming is already bringing hurricanes, floods, and droughts that are more frequent and more violent than any recorded in history, with worse to come.

Clearly, to survive in the long term in a tolerable state, we need to create environments and societies that provide for our biological selves while meeting our psychological, social, and spiritual needs and aspirations. At the same time we need to recognize the physical limits of our landscapes and of the Earth as a whole so that over time the world itself becomes more secure, more fertile, more diverse. We cannot afford, as now, just to run it down.

So how do we achieve this? Clearly we need to do the right kinds of things in the right kinds of ways: we need benign and astute policies, backed by understanding and skill — meaning good science and wisdom, and appropriate craft and technology.

But we never will frame the right policies, or develop the appropriate science and technologies, until and unless we create an economy that promotes such policies and technologies, or at least allows them to happen. The economy is not just a matter of money, as seems commonly to be understood. It is all-pervasive: the matrix and the mechanism of society, the means and the medium through which all our aspirations, our needs, and our deep desires and whims, can be translated into reality. Equally, we need appropriate governance: people and institutions in positions of hands-on power who truly have the well-being of humanity at heart, both material and spiritual, and do not promise more than can possibly be delivered.

In short, right now, across the board, we need Renaissance. We need to think again from first principles about everything we now take for granted. We don't need to "wipe the slate clean" or any other such absolutist nonsense but we do need to take serious stock of all that we have and build afresh on whatever is good and worth rescuing, and let the rest go; not waste time on philosophies and institutions and technologies that can already be seen to be failing. Above all we need to think "holistically" – much abused though that word has been; think about everything in the context of everything else. This, at the moment, is what the world spectacularly fails to do, and so we have buildings that win all the architectural prizes but may be impossible to live in, farming that breaks all records yet fails to feed people, societies that on paper are rich beyond the dreams of Croesus or of Solomon yet wreck their own environment and cause all but a few to be miserable. Most bizarrely, we are ostensibly conducting a "war on poverty" while perpetrating an economy that seems expressly designed to create it.

Above all, we need an economy that works on its own terms and yet is firmly rooted, as the present economy is not, in moral, spiritual, and social values; and is geared, as the present economy is not, to the physical realities of the Earth. There is no shortage of ideas, some of which are still theoretical, although many are already put into practice and known to work. Many of these ideas were developed by various of the twenty-five economists and other thinkers who met over five days in November 2007 at Schumacher College at Dartington, Devon, to discuss what they provisionally called "Holistic Economics".

I was privileged to take part in that think tank, and this is a personal account. I cannot hope to do justice to everyone's ideas – at the very least, as Tariq Banuri of the Stockholm Environment Institute pointed out, the world needs a new textbook of economics just to lay out the new thinking, for the existing ideas that are now being absorbed by the next generation of world leaders are part of the disaster. This is just an interim outline of work in progress. I will focus as the meeting did on the matters that are often the most neglected; on the morality and spirituality; on new economic structures; on the nature of governance; and pick up on just a few particular issues that are especially pressing – money, energy, and food.

How did we get in this mess?

Common sense suggests that if we care about our own wellbeing and the fate of our fellow creatures, then we have to develop an economy that is designed to serve those interests; and if we want the Earth to remain habitable, then we need also to gear that economy to its physical realities.

In practice, the prevailing economy is designed expressly to create wealth, in the apparent belief that if we have enough money, we can always buy our way out of trouble. Political leaders strive above all for "economic growth" – by which they mean increase in Gross Domestic Product or GDP. But GDP is simply a measure of the total money in circulation; and as John Maynard Keynes, no less, pointed out when GDP was still a new concept, it has nothing directly to do with human wellbeing. Above the level of abject poverty, more wealth has remarkably little impact on wellbeing. Yet our whole society is wedded to the ideal of personal accumulation and overall economic growth. Economic growth is bound to be achieved most effectively via a system of economics that is designed expressly to make money. That system is neoliberalism – so that is what we have.

In the neoliberal economy the market is conceived to be global – everyone trading with everyone else – which up to a point is what does actually happen. The global market is intended to be maximally competitive – which it is except when the competition becomes too hot for the biggest players, when they call "foul", and may suspend the rules. There should be no tariffs, trade barriers, quotas or subsidies – apart of course from the subsidies that support US and European agriculture. There must be no cartels – except of course between consenting corporates, which to a significant extent are cartels themselves. The whole caboodle is supported by and depends upon high tech, which by definition includes the kinds of technologies that emerge from science.

Since the results of all these endeavours are so obviously disastrous an objective observer might well conclude that those who support it must either be seriously stupid or seriously wicked. Closer examination would reveal that although some of them surely are, some certainly are not. Many of the keenest economists and scientists have extremely high IQs and many of them want to do good and can see no alternative to more of the same. In practice they are hovering between Voltaire's Dr Pangloss – "All is for the best in this, the best of all possible worlds" and Charles Dickens' Mr Micawber – "Something will turn up!".

In truth, though, the economists and scientists who have created the status quo are not trying to be moralists – either good or bad. Indeed they claim to be morally neutral – and claim, somewhat oxymoronically, that this neutrality is itself a virtue. For, they say, it is not their job to tell the rest of us how we should live our lives. In similar vein the technologists claim that their job is merely to provide — an endless supply of goods that become better and smarter with each generation. We all benefit every day in a thousand ways, from vaccines to mobile 'phones. The free market economists present these goods to the rest of us as if in a global cafeteria – indeed, like the biggest of all possible cornucopias. We, conceived now as "consumers", merely have to choose. "Choice" is the promise of high tech neoliberalism. Choice, in turn, like the free market itself, is equated with freedom in the general sense.

Of course, the neoliberal claims are not true in detail. No-one can choose anything from the cornucopia unless they have money to pay, and the system is such that those who have no money, will stay without; while those who have most money also have the most power, and so dictate what the market provides. Justice is not built in to the system.

Yet the most profound and damaging mistake, made both by the high-technologists who provide the goods and by the free marketeers who pile 'em high and sometimes sell 'em remarkably cheap, lies in their fundamental claim to be morally neutral. But of course they are not. Any action that affects another human being or any living creature of any kind has some moral connotations; and the modern high-tech-neoliberal axis affects all of us profoundly, and the fabric of the world itself. More specifically, the present system perpetrates its own particular values and states of mind. Its values, in the end, are entirely materialistic. The whole complex is designed to provide *stuff* — the more the better. It grinds to a halt unless people consume – more and more and more. This in turn requires universal dissatisfaction – the constant desire not to be a better person, but to own more, and to be seen to own more, for the consumer society works best when people start to measure their own worth as human beings in terms of what they possess.

Take the two together – the enormous, and indeed all-pervasive influence of the present high-tech/ neoliberal economy and the particular values it perpetrates – and the claim to moral neutrality is exposed as the grossest nonsense. Yet the idea of it is bruited from the highest places.

In contrast, those who are advocating the new, "holistic" economics do acknowledge the obvious; that all economic systems must have an ethical agenda, whether its perpetrators realize this or not. Satish Kumar of Schumacher College, one of the think-tank conveners, quotes Gandhi: "To make an economic system without ethics is like churning butter from sand". All agreed that in the new system the moral principles must be explicit. To leave those principles embedded and to fail even to recognize that they exist is, quite simply, ludicrous.

So what are the moral principles that should inform holistic economics?

The path to morality

When conventional economists and scientists do talk ethically, they tend to take a utilitarian position: "Greatest happiness of the greatest number". But since their underlying philosophy is materialist, they tend to see this as an exercise in cost-effectiveness. (I have even heard human cloning defended on the grounds that there will be a market for it, and therefore it must be good. Grotesque but true).

Yet the people who in practice have done most to shape or to make morality explicit are and have always been the great religious teachers. They do not speak in utilitarian terms, and certainly not in materialist terms. Neither, despite what their detractors claim, are they primarily "absolutist" – simply asserting that such-and-such an action is morally right because God says so. To a man and woman, the great teachers are all exponents of "virtue ethics". Sometimes they may frame specific edicts but for most part they are at pains to define *attitude*. We will behave well if we look at ourselves, our fellow creatures, and the universe at large, in the right way. The point is not simply to discuss particular cases but to cultivate attitudes that are appropriate to all.

The great religions differ in their day-to-day edicts – don't eat pork, don't eat beef, whatever; and their detractors seize upon this. But at the fundamental level of virtue ethics, all the great teachers are agreed; and this, in truth, is one of the world's most wondrous serendipities – that all the many different paths, in many different parts of the world and at different times, have led us to the same morality. At the Schumacher meeting, Sulak Sivaraksa of the Santi Pracha Dhamma Institute summarized the Buddhist attitude in one word, as did the Buddha himself: "Compassion". Sulak and others also quoted Jesus who had a different word for the same concept: "Love". Others, including easterners like Satish and westerners like Frances Moore Lappé of the Small Planet Project, Massachusetts, and Miriam Kennet of the Green Economics Institute, Oxford, invoked the ancient concepts of personal humility, respect for all living creatures, and a sense of reverence for the world as a whole. The perpetual sense of dissatisfaction, on which the present economy depends, should give way to a sense of "enoughness".

Should people at large have trouble with this? Do modern people reject religious teaching as a matter of course? There is no reason to think this. The great religions are flourishing and most people when asked claim to have spiritual leanings, even if they do not have particular religious preferences. Certainly, most people demonstrate how much they hate the injustices of the world – and, once they are securely above the breadline, how little they value wealth per se. Almost everyone, when asked, says that they value family, friends and general well-being, far more than any material possessions. The very rich say this as emphatically as anybody. A predominate interest in wealth per se is widely perceived to be the mark of a sociopath. It seems odd, then, to perpetrate an economy that is specifically dedicated to the thing that most of us claim to hold in such little regard.

But is there any other kind of economy? Can we conceive of a viable economy that is *not* rooted in the idea that wealth must be maximized? Well, there are a million and more examples out there already, of folk economies that simply enable societies to tick along, supplying what's needed and leaving time for living. Historically, the present, frenetic materialism and dedication to the god of GDP is an aberration; a madness; a Dawkins-like meme. The competition that is now perceived to be the vital driver, without which we are told the world must grind to a halt, is often replaced by cooperation. Competition, after all, as Satish said, is "violence". Competition means there must be winners and losers; and the vast populations who are now suffering so badly, and the creatures that now face extinction, are simply the losers in a system that is designed to create losers. If we had reverence for the Earth as a whole we surely would not exploit what it has to offer as blithely as we do – and make a virtue of our own rapacity, as in the triumphalist and astonishingly crass: "Man's conquest of Nature!".

But folk economies are one thing, and modernity is another. Can we really envisage a worldwide economy based on non-material values, universal compassion, and cooperativeness? Wouldn't this simply turn us all into hippies and wool-gatherers? The present economy may explode through its own voraciousness, but wouldn't this new, "holistic" economy simply fizzle out?

Why should it? The notion that human beings work only for material gain and to outsmart their neighbours is an obvious nonsense. If it were true then there would be no teachers or nurses and, these days, precious few farmers. We would all be working in the city. The idea that cooperative economies are innately less efficient than competitive economies is answered in many ways (not the least being – what do you mean by "efficiency"?). The decisive answer, though, is provided by the same game theory that is invoked to show the advantage of competitiveness. In one of its simplest forms, game theory explores the relationship between metaphorical hawks (the aggressive ones, keen on acquisition at all costs) and hypothetical doves (pacific, not too demanding, and not fighting back). In any unregulated society, hawks are bound to arise, since there is no-one to stop them arising. Then they bully the doves. So they increase in number. But as the hawks increase then each of them finds as they swagger through life that they keep meeting other hawks. Then they get into fights. So the number of hawks is self-regulating. They increase only until they start making life intolerable for each other.

Inevitably (the theory shows) all societies left to themselves are liable in the end to be mixed – with both doves and hawks. Always, the theory suggests, the peaceable doves are liable to outnumber the aggressive hawks: a plausible ratio is 80 doves for every 20 hawks. But always, the hawk minority will rule, because the doves let them.

Now apply some arithmetic of a utilitarian kind: measure the wellbeing/happiness of each individual in the standard, mixed society with a score out of 10. Assuming that the hawks like being hawks, then in a mixed society each hawk scores 10. If there are 20 hawks, their total score is 200. The doves, meanwhile – 80 of them – average only 4 apiece, so their total happiness score is 320. The total for the whole, mixed society, is 520. In a society where there are no hawks, no-one gets to do exactly what he or she likes, so no individual can achieve a maximum happiness score above 8. But since all are equal, all score 8. So the total happiness score for the whole society is 800. Of course the arithmetic is crude and the assumptions are cavalier but the general principle is surely true. Most obviously, in a cooperative society, no-one wastes time and energy in fighting.

Present-day politicians like to argue, of course, and some of them sincerely believe, that they have the best interests of the people at heart. They would like to maximize total happiness – but they are also wedded to the notion of maximizing GDP, which has little to do with happiness. It is easy to envisage societies in which GDP is maximized by destroying the environment (cutting down the forest, polluting the rivers in the search for gold); wrecking local societies (the people who rely on the forest, or fished in the rivers); in which all the new wealth finishes up in the hands of the (hawkish) minority; and is then used to make changes that create yet more havoc for the poor majority (tourist hotels in place of coastal villages, and so on and so on). In fact such examples are all around us. The oil-rich countries are fabulously wealthy yet are home to some of the world's most put-upon people. We should be measuring success, said Satish, not by gross domestic *product* but by Gross National *happiness*. Bhutan has already introduced this as a principle. So far the US has not put a stop to it, presumably because Bhutan is not on any strategic route. The world as a whole would do well to follow Bhutan.

There is one final irony. The Schumacher workshop that discussed these issues arrived at this idea – gross national happiness rather than GDP – by rejecting utilitarian ethics in favour of virtue ethics. But simple game theory shows that an economy driven by compassion and the desire to cooperate produces more wellbeing than the one that sets out to be utilitarian. Buddha and Jesus were other-worldly. But game theory suggests that they were good economists, too.

But let us look more closely at the present economy. It serves us badly for the general reason that it is so inveterately materialist and competitive. Yet its shortcomings are compounded by some serious structural flaws – which, unfortunately, very few people understand including, it seems, many of the world's leaders.

Chapter 2

The Money Renaissance

The present world needs radical repair. Tinkering will not do. Yet it is a huge mistake to be more radical than we need to be. If we simply rush in, weapons drawn, then we will waste effort, destroy institutions and systems that could have been put to good use, pick fights that we do not need to have, turn potential friends into enemies, and in the end will probably fail.

So we must first address a meta-question: how radical do we need to be? In some ways the economic ideas proposed at Schumacher (some of them developed by their proponents over several decades) seem startling. Yet they are far from wild. It may well be that we need to address the specific issue of land-ownership; but nobody is saying, for example, as Joseph-Pierre Proudhon did in the late 19th century, "All property is theft". Barter has a role in the new economy – but no-one wants to revert to a stone-age economy. Unfettered corporates with a brief and a mandate simply to get richer do not serve the world well – but no-one is suggesting, like some of the successors of Karl Marx, that everything should be owned and controlled by the state. In fact all the most obvious trappings of capitalism in the broad sense can be left in place – money, private ownership, private enterprise (although, to re-emphasise, land ownership does need to be addressed). Capitalism doesn't have to mean what it has come to mean – the neo-liberal, global, competitive but nonetheless contrived generation of wealth, which in practice is dominated by the most powerful players, who are the corporates and the governments who serve and are served by those corporates. But because so many people now equate capitalism with the neo-liberal global market, a new economy that is significantly different needs a new name. Even so, the new systems are rooted in principles that traditional businesspeople would certainly recognize. In short: the changes now proposed are certainly radical – probably radical enough – but they need not gratuitously frighten the horses.

Many of the world's problems, as Margrit Kennedy of MonNetA in

Steyerberg, Germany, has been expounding for the past 25 years, spring from one of the economy's most basic components: compound interest.

Compound interest seems logical enough. We take it for granted that when we borrow money, we must pay interest, to compensate the lender for their trouble and kindness. It seems logical, too, that this should be compound interest. It seems only fair. If we borrow £100 at 3% interest p.a., then at the end of the first year we should pay back £103. But if we fail to pay the £103 after one year, then at the end of the second year we must also pay interest on the £103 that should have been paid.

This may seem innocuous enough, but it has immense consequences. The debt increases exponentially. The problem does not show up immediately. Three per cent of £103 is not much more than three per cent of £100. But at 3% compound interest, a debt left unpaid will double in 24 years. At 6% – a more realistic rate – the debt doubles every 12 years. At 12%, the debt doubles every 6 years. Even when the rate seems innocuous a debt can soon become so great that no-one can ever pay it off. Over the past few decades the countries of the Third World have found this out to their cost. In 2000, after the G8 Summit in Okinawa, President Obasonjo of Nigeria wanly remarked that "All that we borrowed up to 1985 or 1986 was about $5 billion. So far we have paid back about $16 billion. Yet we're being told that we still owe about $28 billion ... because of foreign creditors' interest rates". He added, "If you ask me what is the worst thing in the world, I will say it is compound interest".

On the smaller scale (but it matters), post-grads in Britain now begin their careers owing the cost of their education. Some post-docs in the US, like many a Third World country, can never pay off those debts, unless sanity and common humanity again prevail and acknowledge the nonsense. The economy in this form is not the servant of humanity. Instead, the economy determines how we must live, and what we must aim for – what our attitudes should be, and indeed what kind of people we are obliged to become. Post-grads in serious debt cannot afford to be social workers. They must join the race and get rich quick. A country in deep debt cannot spend its energies on planting trees or on health-care. But that is what foreign aid is for, isn't it? Well, in 2000, the developing world was spending 13 dollars on debt repayment for every one dollar it received in aid and grants.

Surely, though, if you want to avoid paying compound interest, you should simply avoid getting into debt? Shouldn't we just resolve to live within our means, as traditional people traditionally did? But in our present economy you will always be paying the interest on somebody else's debts even if you are not ostensibly in debt yourself. For very few people can produce things these days without borrowing money first (most farmers certainly cannot). So the price of everything you buy includes whatever the producer owes to his creditors – paid at compound interest. The trickle is inexorable.

Which leads us to the greatest iniquity of all. In Germany, said Margrit – and Germany is in general a stable and in many ways enviable modern society — about 80% of the people, the simple kind who make their living by working, pay out about twice as much in interest each year as they receive from their various investments. About 10 per cent of the people are in balance; they are receiving roughly as much in interest from their various investments as they are paying out just through buying things. The remaining 10 per cent are net beneficiaries – receiving all the interest paid out by the 80 per cent who are the net payers. Thus it was that in Germany in 2004 about one billion euros *every day* found their way from the 80 per cent who work for a living to the 10 per cent who sit at the top of the financial tree. The equivalent rate of transfer in Britain seems likely to be even higher since most people here have a mortgage and mortgages on average account for half our disposable income. Globally, absurdly, the governments of rich nations have declared a "war on poverty" while presiding over an economic system in which the rich are bound to grow inexorably richer while the poor grow poorer.

Margrit did not say that this kind of an economic structure is systematic theft, but I will say it. Successive governments vie to be harsher and harsher on "crime" and use taxpayers' money to build bigger and bigger jails or else build them with private enterprise and leave the taxpayers with the debts. Yet the governments themselves preside over larceny on the grandest scale. Compared with this, Al Capone was a playground bully. That this larceny is legal makes it worse. When the law itself is on the side of obvious injustice, then we really have something to worry about. Margrit claims that few understand how this works. People surely would not tolerate such nonsense if they realized the enormity of it – and neither presumably would most politicians care to preside over it.

Overall, compound interest creates debt that can in principle be of infinite proportions. The debt represents money, so it seems as if the world's money is potentially infinite. But money is supposed to be exchangeable for goods and services – and the fabric of the world is all too obviously finite, while in practice there is only a limited number of services that human beings can carry out for each other, at least of any useful kind. So this infinitely expanding pool of money is in truth a bubble – and one, of course, that could be popped at any time. Pertinent here is a much quoted line from John Maynard Keynes from 1936: "Speculators may do no harm as bubbles on a steady stream of enterprise. But the position is serious when enterprise becomes the bubble on a whirlpool of speculation. When the capital development of a country becomes a by-product of the activities of a casino, the job is likely to be ill-done." "The by-product of a casino" – seems like a very good description of the present world economy. Indeed, the British government's recent and mercifully brief flirtation with literal, mega-casinos was a potent symbol.

All this is weird – but it gets weirder, as the London-based economist Ann Pettifor has shown. For although most of us know – of course we do – that modern banks do not literally keep chests of doubloons and pieces of eight to lend out to their clientele, most of us do seem to feel, deep down, that *something* like this applies. That is, we assume (because it seems only reasonable) that the bank that lends us £100,000, say, to buy a house, actually *has* £100,000, even if this money does not literally exist in the form of sovereigns.

This is far from the case. In reality, the commercial banks from whom we borrow do not hold, and (as the law stands) do not have to hold, anything like the amount that they are prepared to lend to us. After all, if you borrow £100,000 for a house, you don't mean that you want that much *cash*. You do not expect to walk away with a wheelbarrow full of actual specie. Instead, the money is transferred into your account, and thence is noiselessly and invisibly transferred to the account of whoever you are buying the house from. In fact the money does not have to exist at all. It is merely deemed to exist. The bank does, however, by law, have to hold an amount in cash that is a *proportion* of the amount it lends out – but only a small proportion.

So here's how it works. You ask the commercial bank for £100,000. The commercial bank then asks the central bank – say, the Bank of England – for a quantity of cash equivalent to the amount of cash that it (the commercial bank) is obliged to hold to back up your loan. This might be around £5000. On the back of this, the commercial bank can then lend you the £100,000. Once the figures have gone into the ledger (or been registered on the appropriate computer chip) the money is deemed to have changed hands, even though it never really existed.

Now the really smart bit. The commercial bank has borrowed only £5000 (in cash) from the central bank, so it pays (compound) interest only on £5000. This it pays at "the bank rate" – say 5%. But you have borrowed (or are deemed to have borrowed) £100,000 from the commercial bank, and you have to pay compound interest on all of it; and you will pay above the bank rate – say 7%.

When you have your mortgage you go away feeling very pleased – now you have a home to live in. To be sure, from now on you probably have to pay about half your disposable income to the bank (this is roughly the average in Britain) – but you feel grateful to them nonetheless for helping you out of a hole; envisaging (deep down) that they have somehow depleted their stocks by digging in to the treasure chest, albeit a hypothetical treasure chest.

Yet the bank has done no such thing. It has merely taken out a small loan with the central bank at a favourable rate, and then written a few lines in a ledger or two or pressed a few computer keys. The money that it is deemed to have lent you is notional. It was conjured into existence by your agreement to repay it, not with hypothetical money but with real money, on 7% at compound interest, for 20 or 25 years – or until you die, when the bank will repossess what is then deemed to be their share. Nice work if you can get it.

This modus operandi sounds pretty grotesque when private individuals are involved. When governments start borrowing money on the same kind of terms we are truly in fantasy land. For there is no a priori reason why the government itself should not own the bank. If it did, then it could take out as much money as it needed without paying interest at all. Governments these days are forever telling us that they cannot "afford" to do things that obviously need doing. Ann Pettifor cites the government of Tanzania, which said when she was last there that it could not "afford" to buy rubber gloves for midwives. In Britain there is a shortage not of rubber gloves but of the midwives themselves, or so it is widely reported. Yet the British government assures us it has spent a fortune on health care and cannot possibly "afford" more. But as Keynes pointed out some decades ago, governments in truth could "afford" to do anything – if only they did not lock themselves into systems which ensure that they (meaning the taxpayers) must pay the lion's share to banks for conjuring money into existence out of the ether.

All this may sound too bizarre to be even half-way plausible – yet this is how things work nonetheless. The people who have drawn attention to its peculiarities include that minority of mainstream economists and businesspeople who really understand the system — including, over the past century, Keynes, Henry Ford, and Thomas Edison. Or as Josiah Charles Stamp (1880 – 1941) put the matter: "The modern banking system manufactures money out of nothing. The process is perhaps the most astounding piece of sleight-of-hand that was ever invented". Stamp was no loony-lefty. In the 1920s he was President of the Bank of England, and the second richest man in Great Britain.

Oddly enough, the system *could* work for the benefit of people as a whole. If any of us wants to begin any new enterprise, a shop or a farm or a workshop for mending violins, we first need the cash to set ourselves up. In the olden days, as the Belgian economist Bernard Lietaer points out, we would either have to work most of our working life to earn the cash to enable us to start the work we really want to do, or else go cap in hand to some rich patron who might be prepared to pay-roll us in return for some favour. Nowadays we can achieve the same end without such hoops. There is a central pool of cash — albeit a virtual pool of cash – safeguarded by the banks, on which any of us is free to draw provided only we can show our ability to pay it back. By borrowing money that does not exist we create a debt, to be sure. But the debt is made good by the work we do subsequently, using the money we have borrowed. The whole system is based on trust. If the money is lent responsibly, and the borrowers meet their promises, all is well. If the borrower fails, or reneges, then the debt should in the end be made good by the collective endeavours of the whole society; so it's as if all of society is investing in the dreams and aspirations of each individual who wants to borrow. But if such a system is to truly work in the interests of the society as a whole, then the guardians of the central, virtual pool of money should be seen as public servants; paid a good wage for their competence but not expected to gain otherwise. But this is not what happens. Under the present system the guardians of the pool are the chief beneficiaries. How did that happen? The general answer is that the economy has lost touch with its social, moral roots; and, for good measure, has lost touch in its virtual world with the physical realities of the finite Earth.

Clearly, if we want to put things right – if we want a world in which moral principles and physical realities can again take precedence over the fantasies of modern money – then we need to dig deep. Many different devices are in the offing – some already up and running – and among the most significant is that of complementary currencies: discussed at the Schumacher meeting mainly by Margrit Kennedy, Richard Douthwaite who works out of County Mayo in Eire, and Bernard Lietaer.

Complementary currencies are what the term implies: currencies that operate in parallel with national currencies, and perform functions that national currencies can carry out only clumsily, and sometimes not at all. In principle they may come in many forms – from the very small scale to the largest. Thus they include the local currencies that are now being issued in Britain for example by "transition towns", such as Totnes and Stroud. In Germany, more than 400 complementary currencies are in operation. Bernard Lietaer, working in Brazil, has shown how such a complementary currency can operate in education. Seven-year-olds are given £200 (say) in education vouchers. These they use to pay older children (whom they choose for themselves) to coach them in their weaker subjects. The older children – say 11-year-olds – then pay 12-year-olds to coach them; and so on all the way up. The 17-year-olds, at the top of the tree, then pass on the cash that they have received from the class below to their universities – who then re-convert the vouchers into cash. Thus the same, inflation-proof, notional £200 may be re-used up to ten times or more, and buys ten times or more teaching time than it otherwise would. Children, incidentally, can be excellent teachers – and they too gain because the best way to learn (as has been demonstrated) is by teaching.

One of the greatest requirements of all, however, is to re-ground money in reality. Until 1971 cash corresponded to gold – "the gold standard" – until, that is, Richard Nixon unilaterally detached the dollar. Since then currencies have "floated" – their value determined by "the market".

This, as Bernard points out, produces one of the weirdest anomalies of all. For we take it for granted, do we not, that all units of measurement should be standardized. The kilogram, the second, the metre – all are defined to the nth decimal place by reference to some unchangeable feature of the universe. The only units that are not fixed, are those of currency: the thing which in practice, more than anything, determines how we live. Money in the modern economy is innately unstable – and there is huge vested interest in keeping it so, because one of the ways to get really really rich is simply by changing one form of currency that happens to be doing well into another form that happens to be doing badly, and then do the opposite when the fortunes reverse. So it is that $1.3 *trillion* are traded in the foreign exchange markets every day. Nearly 96% of these transactions is purely speculative, in no way reflecting the global movement or exchange of actual goods or services. But although all this shifting money is airy-fairy its effect is immense precisely because in theory at any second it can, in principle, be re-converted into reality. Bernard, like Margrit, is apt to observe like Keynes that our present economy is indeed a bubble.

So Bernard is seeking to re-ground the world's currencies in reality: the "Trade Reference Currency", or TRC. Its unit is the Terra. Its value is calculated according to a "basket" of about a dozen real commodities of inescapable worth. The contents of the basket would vary according to their market value – but because each one is balanced against the others the value remains constant and inflation-proof. Thus, at any one time, 100 Terras might be deemed to be equivalent to one barrel of oil plus five bushels of wheat, ten pounds of copper and three of tin, one tenth of an ounce of gold, one Carbon Emission Right – and so on.

No government would care or be able to create the TRC, said Bernard. It would have to be a private issue, from a private bank. Therefore by definition it would be a "complementary currency". So we see that complementary currencies need not be small-scale but could be major players in the world economy, and a very significant stabilizing force. Neither is the TRC just pie in the sky. Some senior executives of very large companies are taking the idea very seriously. A rough precedent is already provided by countertrade – formal bartering on the international scale. For example, Pepsi-cola from the US is traded on a fairly substantial scale for Stolichnaya vodka from Russia. Both have unequivocal value whatever may happen to the dollar or the ruble. The Terra could, however, serve as a universal token in any such exchange – which is what money is supposed to be for.

So the world needs a Renaissance – an economic Renaissance. The ideas outlined here – just a taste of what there is — are not fanciful. They could all happen. The main obstacles are inertia and, perhaps most of all, vested interest. Innately unstable currencies are mostly bad for most of us and sometimes disastrous – Bernard Lietaer has listed 87 major currency crises worldwide over the past 20 years. But if you want to be really really rich then you should not waste your time making things, or teaching, or ministering to the sick. Just play one currency off against another. Even some of the really rich are not happy with this. As the billionaire, the late James Goldsmith, put the matter, "I feel I have won a game of poker on board *The Titanic*. Why should I want even more money when I will just be surrounded by more and more poor and suffering people who hate me?" But some people are very content with the status quo; and in an age in which money is the arbiter of all things the people who are really really rich have corresponding influence.

The new economics does need a new name, however, to distinguish it from the status quo and all that has passed before. "Holistic economics" was the working title of the meeting – but some felt that "holistic" now has too many connotations of its own. Satish suggested "naturalism" – economics intended to protect nature, just as capitalism is intended to protect capital. He also mooted the Sanskrit *sarvodaya* meaning "rising up" or "all rise", a term much favoured by Gandhi. I quite like "Enlightened Economics" to match "Enlightened Agriculture", as discussed later – with connotations both of European rationalism and of Buddhist insight. But this was not resolved.

More to the point: how might the new principles apply to present problems?

Some crucial practicalities: energy and farming

Since everything is related to everything else, we might start a discussion of what we should be doing from any point. We could begin with child health; with housing; with women's rights; with the provision of fresh water; with pollution; with the mass extinction of species. All are in need of radical appraisal, all of them have to be got right, and each in the end leads us into all of the others.

But as George Orwell might have put the matter, some considerations seem more equal than others; and at the heart of all human affairs – and therefore, since human beings have such a big impact on the world, at the heart of all worldly affairs – are the energy supply, and agriculture. Each is properly perceived as a *sine qua non*. Get them right, and the world has some chance of enduring in a tolerable form – or indeed in a positively agreeable form. Get either of them wrong, and everything else that we might aspire to do is compromised. At the moment we are getting both of them so horribly wrong that even our survival beyond the next few decades seems far from certain.

Chapter 3

The Energy Renaissance

The Industrial Revolution was fired by what seemed like a "free" resource: first coal and then oil. So we gobbled them up as quickly as they could be mined and drilled. So we have become completely dependent upon them. But nothing is for nothing. First they caused horrible and often lethal pollution in the form of soot and acid – problems that can be solved, now, although there is still a long way to go. Now the oil, by far the most convenient resource, is running out. We are reaching "peak oil" – an expression that seems to be defined in various ways but in its simplest form implies that demand is continuing to rise, exponentially, while productivity is leveling out; and we will never produce much more than we do now because no-one has found any seriously big new oil-fields for some time and there may not be any.

Worst of all, though, is that when fossil fuels are burnt the carbon they contain is oxidized to carbon dioxide. Plants and rocks absorb surplus CO_2 but their capacity to do so is limited; and if their limit is exceeded, the CO_2 accumulates in the atmosphere. Since 1750 the concentration of CO_2 in the atmosphere has risen from 280 ppm (parts per million) to 380 ppm – and the responsibility seems to lie mainly with the world's new mills, factories, power stations, cars, ships, planes, trains, and its increasingly industrialized agriculture. CO_2 is the chief of the "greenhouse gases", which prevent the escape of radiant heat (infra-red) from the Earth's surface, and so the world is warming up. Global temperature rose by 0.7 degrees C in the 20th century which may not sound much, but is already causing serious and obvious changes – hurricanes, droughts, and floods that are more frequent and severe than have ever been recorded. Climate scientists suggest that if atmospheric CO_2 is allowed to rise above 500 ppm then the whole world could be in serious trouble. Much more than that would result in serious collapse.

In fact, as Tariq Banuri commented in a recent paper**, the fossil fuels were not "free" at all. The astonishing accumulation of CO_2 represents a "debt" which, now, we have to start repaying as quickly as possible – "through the reduction of emissions below the steady state level for several decades or centuries". How?

Some have suggested that "peak oil" will solve the greenhouse problem: if there is no more oil to burn, then we cannot push out any more surplus CO_2. But there is easily enough oil left in the ground to push the world into a virtually terminal phase if we burn it too fast – and besides, before the oil runs out the world is liable to turn to coal and various oil-rich shales, which produce just as much CO_2. Various technical fixes have been proposed including "carbon fixing" – sending carbon dioxide underground to bind with various rocks; but as with all such schemes, this is easier said than done (and there are many trillions of tonnes of CO_2 to dispose of). Nuclear power brings its own problems and besides, uranium in the end is a non-renewable resource, just as fossil fuels are. Once the uranium is gone it's gone. Nuclear fusion, of the kind that powers the Sun, is still a dream. Of the possible renewables, the "alternative" most popular with governments is biofuel, but fuel crops need land that is needed for food – and is also needed by other species. Various forms of solar power – including that of wind and waves – and tidal power offer more realistic alternatives. But whatever technologies we come up with we must, if we are serious, contrive to keep as much carbon as possible in the ground, locked up in oil and coal. Again: How?

One immediate approach is for everyone simply to use less energy; and one obvious way – and in practice, usually, the most cost-effective – is to waste less. We might therefore suppose that governments that were alert to the issues and felt it was their job to govern would be offering incentives to their citizens to do just this, with copious expert advice. Britain's government, however, is doing no such thing. Antony Turner is helping to fill the gap with his not-for-profit Foundation, "CarbonSense" which, he says, aims to 'accelerate society's shift to a low-carbon future'. CarbonSense Ltd helps senior people in companies such as BT and TNT truly to understand the issues – not just from a business perspective, but

---

** "Climate Change and Sustainable Development, Tariq Banuri and Hans Opschoor, DESA Working Paper No 56, October 2007.

also personally. CarbonSense always works with the culture of the business – "but in a way that challenges and provokes. This means that the business managers start to take decisions that they feel 'make sense' from a climate change perspective".

Antony believes that western society needs to rapidly move towards a different level of understanding – what he calls 'carbon literacy'. "The science is getting tougher and more compelling – there is no doubt we are changing the atmosphere of the planet and the bit we are changing is the bit that controls the temperature. The challenge," he says, "is to get a billion people carbon literate within five years."

In the longer term, he says, we – the world – must contrive to derive all our energy from renewable resources. Although he hates to use the word "should" he has no doubt that if the world is to survive then all of us need to be prepared to pay more for our energy, in absolute terms and as a proportion of income – and also pay a higher price for all products and services, including food, to reflect their true carbon costs. Higher prices are needed to encourage more efficient use, and this in turn will provide the incentive that business needs to become more energy efficient and turn to renewable energy.

The best arrangements for creating and distributing energy in the future have yet to evolve, but we already have pointers. Mutually-owned and locally controlled Energy Services Companies surely have a serious role to play. Offshore wind and tidal generators could supply significant energy long-distance, internationally. In short, again, the beginnings of solutions seem to be out there, organizationally and technically. It's just a question of making them happen.

So why aren't they happening already on the grand scale? "Key barriers" include a general lack of awareness (still) of both climate change / carbon and peak oil; and huge problems in adapting or renewing present energy supply systems, which were built at a time when energy was cheap and seemed destined to last forever. Poorly insulated houses and bad planning are part of the issue. There is also opposition to local grids, and in practice there are very few examples of local community energy systems that are up and running. Key, too, is that the major greenhouse gases do not impinge directly on our senses. They are invisible and without odour. People in all walks of life clearly find it hard to conceive that they are so potent. We need, says Antony Turner, to make carbon in its gaseous forms "visible in the landscape of our lives".

We would surely do well to establish a high price for carbon – and make sure that the price remains stable for years to come; not just leave it to fluctuate, as is the modern way, according to market whim or government expediency. We need much more advice at the local level. The path for communities who do set up such schemes should be smoothed — for example with laws that made it easy for local generating groups to feed in to the grid, and offered an attractive tariff. This is done in many countries such as Germany where the 'feed-in' tariff system provides incentive for the production of local renewable energy. At the moment those who want to do good and necessary things must first jump through rows of bureaucratic hoops. Again though, says Antony, "I think the challenge is that most people, and that includes Civil Servants, genuinely don't understand the problem. Civil Servants generally don't like change –so it is quite reasonable for them to hold back when they are not convinced of the need for change. The UK has provided much of the science – but the necessary change is agonizingly slow in relation to the speed of response that scientists are asking for".

Tariq Banuri approaches the issues at a global level. Most importantly, he says, present policies to cope with the energy crises have become divorced from, and to some extent are at loggerheads with, the goals of development. In general, enlightened people acknowledge that the developing world needs more industry and a higher standard of living and therefore needs to use more energy; and some observers do acknowledge that people in the developed world use far more energy than they need to (and indeed waste a good deal). To a large extent, then, policy-makers have focused on the need for rich countries to reduce. There is emphasis, too, of course, on the need for poor countries to avoid the mistakes of the western industrial revolution, and to develop the cleanest possible technologies from the word go. Carbon trading is one device intended both to encourage more frugality in the North, and to encourage clean technologies in the South: rich companies that use more energy than they should are invited to pay a tithe to poor countries (analogous perhaps with the Catholic concept of the "indulgence") to help them develop clean technologies. But there are obvious snags with carbon trading. Does it really encourage rich countries to change their ways, or merely to ease their consciences? Is the money that they pay to developing countries really used in the ways that are needed?

Tariq's approach is more radical – derived not least from ideas proposed by the Indian thinkers, Anil Agarwal and Sunita Narain, in 2001.

Clearly, global warming is a global problem. The atmosphere knows no national or economic boundaries. Whatever happens in one place, affects everybody. So it is very much in the interests of the North to help the South to move towards "de-carbonization" with all possible speed. Surprising though it may seem, the developing countries already generate more greenhouse gas than the industrial countries – and their output is increasing far faster. In addition, they have far less industrial inertia – to a large extent they are starting from scratch. So investment in the South is liable to be far more cost effective than investment in the North. To put it crudely, the world could get far more de-carbonization to the dollar by investing in the South, than in the North. So Tariq proposes a mega investment fund run at international level, providing direct help on an appropriate scale – meaning a large scale — towards a cleaner future.

This, morally speaking, would require nothing more than enlightened self-interest. Altruism is not required. Whatever helps the South, helps everybody. But – unlike some exercises in enlightened self-interest – this one would be of genuine and immediate help to the South as well, since it would also aid development. Economic growth by unacceptable means to unacceptable ends is crass. But growth that truly is intended to improve well-being, and is achieved by means that are not destructive, is vital. True investment in clean development is surely a key way forward.

Chapter 4

The Food Renaissance

Agriculture sits at the heart of all human affairs. We might summarize all human activity in a diptych: agriculture in one panel, and everything else that we do in the other. It ought to be the thing that all governments take most seriously. But clearly they do not. In Britain, successive governments this past twenty years have seriously wondered if they should get rid of farming all together, just as they got rid of mining, and buy what we need from Africa or Brazil or wherever. Despite all that is happening, some people in the Treasury still think that way. Such pondering in high places shows how decisively, and terrifyingly, the people with most influence in the world have lost touch with reality.

In truth, it should be technically almost easy to feed everyone who is ever liable to be born on to this planet to the highest standards of nutrition (as defined by nutritionists) and of gastronomy (which each culture should define for itself, according to local possibilities and traditions). That means 6.5 billion people need feeding now, and nine billion by 2050. If the population were to go on rising as it has been doing this past ten thousand years (exponentially, in fact, with a few blips here and there) then the task would quickly become impossible. But the United Nations demographers tell us that the percentage rate of increase is declining, and that by 2050 it will have dropped to zero; which means that the human population should stabilize around 2050. This is the greatest ecological shift, and the best news, that the planet has experienced over the past 10,000 years. It means that for the first time since farming became the norm, the task of feeding humanity can be seen to be finite. It is also eminently possible – even with present technologies – to feed that nine billion. The constant, dinning plea for the particular high technology of genetic engineering – GMOs – is yet another example of muddled thinking and vested interest in high places. The demographic projection suggests that the population should stay at around nine billion for a few centuries, and then start to decline. So the task is to prepare to feed nine billion — to a high standard – and then go on doing so for a few hundred years. After that, the task should get easier. Of course it is do-able; and since it can be done it is surely a serious sin of omission – wicked, in fact – not to give it a try.

So how can we provide good food for so many people? The answer is ridiculously simple. *We just have to design agriculture expressly to feed people.* We should and could do this, furthermore, without cruelty to livestock, without perpetrating the mass extinction of other species, without wrecking the environment (including the climate) while, at the same time, creating jobs that are fulfilling to do and communities that are agreeable to live in. Farming is my own personal hobby-horse and I call the kind that is designed expressly to feed people, without foul collateral damage, and with direct benefits to human communities, "Enlightened Agriculture".

So how do we go about this?

In truth, "Enlightened Agriculture" is a high-falutin' term for good sound husbandry and common sense – but abetted, crucially, by science. Absolutely not is it an exercise in nostalgia. Agriculture is and must remain a craft industry, in truth incorporating a host of skills and expertise. But every human activity can benefit from sympathetic science. One of the huge mistakes of the modern world is to use science for a quite different purpose – just to create yet more wealth. With this imperative firmly in mind, agriculture has become more and more industrialized. Agricultural science that is directly or independently paid for by us all is not used to help good farmers to feed us well. It is used to replace those farmers with heavy machinery, industrial chemistry, and biotech. Science properly used, like money properly used, is one of humanity's greatest assets. Science misused, like money misused, is perhaps our most potent enemy.

Good husbandry and common sense means that we should start from biological principles (which include ecological principles). We can begin with the observation (crude, but we have to start somewhere) that the basic task is to produce plenty of food energy ("calories"), with a good though not excessive dose of protein.

This is done most readily by growing staple crops – the term "staple" implies just this: the provision of basic nourishment. Staples include seeds such as the cereals (which are grasses), the pulses (peas, beans, and so on) and nuts (such as coconuts); plus stem and root tubers of various kinds (potatoes, cassava, yams, and so on). In practice, it turns out, just three cereals – wheat, rice, and maize (which the Americans call "corn") – supply all humanity with half of all our energy and two thirds of our protein. It is a surprising statistic, but it seems to be the case.

In general, though not invariably, the staple crops are grown on the field scale: the whole field is ploughed and prepared and the seed is sown en masse. This is "arable" farming. Since the staples are so important the message is: get the arable right and it is all over bar the shouting (or at least you are well over half-way there). So use the best land for arable. Farmers know this: but in careless societies the world over people nowadays tend to build on the best land – because land that is easy to grow crops on tends to be easy to build on too, and so it is cheaper. (But of course the person who buys the house still has to pay through the nose because the price of land and of construction is bumped up by the debt economy).

Arable, though, is not the whole of farming. As St Matthew observed in a slightly different context, "Man does not live by bread alone" (Ch. 4 v. 4). People also need succulence, flavour, texture – plus vitamins, minerals, and that growing list of recondite organic molecules that are now sometimes called "nutraceuticals" but might well be called "paravitamins". These are best supplied by fruit and vegetables – which traditionally are grown on the garden scale, often plant-by-plant, by the methods classed as "horticulture".

With arable and horticulture in place we really have cracked it. Human beings clearly can do well on a well-balanced vegan diet. Yet we don't have to be vegans, or any kind of vegetarian. For although plants produce far more protein and energy per hectare than livestock can do – at least three times as much; and usually ten or even hundred times more – this does *not* mean that an all-plant agriculture is more efficient than one that incorporates livestock judiciously. Ruminants – cows and sheep and a few others – are strict herbivores, which means they do very well on grass and "browse" (the leaves and branches of trees) and so they can be raised on hills and in semi-deserts and woods and even in marshes where arable farming and horticulture are well-nigh impossible. So the ruminants extend the total area that can be used. The omnivorous livestock – pigs and poultry – can be fed, and traditionally always have been fed, on crop surpluses and leftovers, which all farms and all human communities are bound to produce. So the arable farms and the gardens (and orchards) produce even more with a few chickens and ducks and pigs around the place. This of course is what you see in every traditional agrarian society that has not been black-jacked by the modern economy and what is now called "development".

So farming that is designed to feed people produces a great many plants and some, though not much, livestock. To make the whole system work, too, the farms should be mixed and varied; many different crops, and various classes of livestock at different stages of growth, all carefully integrated, so that they all enhance the others. The whole is supplemented by local herbs and wild fruits and nuts – which are not just caprice: they are prime sources of micronutrients (and of course of flavour).

So enlightened agriculture produces plenty of plants, not much meat, and maximum variety.

Which leads us to two wondrous serendipities. First, those nine words – "plenty of plants, not much meat, and maximum variety" – summarize all of the best nutritional theory of the past thirty years. All the surveys and researches and vast literature can be boiled down to this. Hence, the farming that is designed simply to get the best out of the land, and to provide *enough*, also meets our nutritional needs as well as can be devised.

Yet there is more. The great cuisines of the world are of course immensely various, but they have a common core. At the heart of all the greatest cooking – Provence, Italy, Turkey, North Africa, India, China – we find "plenty of plants, not much meat, and maximum variety". The Turks make fabulous banquets from wheat, pistachios, almonds, olive oil, mint, honey – and if a goat happens to have died that week, then it will be included too. Meat in traditional cuisines is not the centerpiece of every meal. It becomes the centerpiece on feast days – but they are occasional. Otherwise it serves only as garnish (epitomized by Chinese cooking) or for stock (of which the Italians are surely the supreme masters).

In short: agriculture that is designed to feed people does not require us even to be austere. Rather the opposite. People who take food seriously, like the traditional southern Italians, are far easier to feed than people who simply want burgers and Kentucky fried. The counterpart of enlightened agriculture is the food culture. The Slow Food Movement, which began in Italy and is now extending worldwide, is one of the most important initiatives of the modern world. The future does not belong to the ascetic. In fact the opposite is the case: the future belongs to the gourmet. Traditional cultures worldwide – those that still exist – already show what can be achieved when sound husbandry is wedded to a true love of food – but all are under threat. Thus Nadia Johanisova describes much that is fine, sustainable and agreeable, in traditional Czechoslovakia. But the modern Czech Republic, like all of eastern Europe, is rapidly being brought into the EU fold. Of course traditional farming is not perfect – but it is amenable to improvement. The modern industrial kind simply has to be re-thought from first principles.

So the future could still be glorious – if only we did simple things well. The necessary skills are all out there. They can be enhanced by science, to be sure, but in truth they arose in peasant fields and kitchens, sometimes thousands of years ago. They show the genius that is in all humanity.

But in the present world we don't do simple things well, because of the economy. The modern economy, indeed, is obliging us to farm very badly indeed – inadequately, dangerously, destructively. But such is the nonsense into which we have succumbed, that the dangerous practices are the ones that are advocated from on high, and actively impressed on people who at the moment are doing things well (at least in principle). So far have we drifted into fantasy, indeed, that the people with most influence in the world now tell us that the measures that are so obviously required to keep the world intact – good farming and good cooking – are "unrealistic".

The rot set in in the 1970s. Then, we first heard the chill expression, "Agriculture is just a business like any other". We need have no fear that agriculture is a "business" – when business is sensibly defined. But nowadays, for "business", read "neoliberalism": a to-the-death competitive global scrabble to generate as much money as possible. That, in the context of agriculture, is very dangerous indeed.

For to maximize the cash return the producer – whatever he or she is producing — needs to do three things: maximize turnover (the stuff that is for sale); "add value" (maximize the gap between the cost of production and the selling price); and minimize costs. Perhaps, when these three principles are crudely applied to computers or to battleships the world benefits – perhaps we finish up with better computers or battleships. Clearly, though, when this crude business imperative is applied to farming, the results are disastrous. We can see the disaster all around us.

First, for agriculture, maximization of turnover means maximizing yield. This can be sensible. If you are practicing horticulture under glass, for instance – which is a perfectly reasonable thing to do – then you have to invest a great deal of capital, and you cannot possibly recoup that capital without growing the crops very intensively indeed. You may control the pests in the glasshouse by biological means and fertilize organically but still you need maximum yield. I have been in modern glasshouses the world over in which the yields beggar belief. You have to jostle your way through the vines of melons and tomatoes, and provided the flavour and texture are not sacrificed – which need not be the case — why not?

But the bulk of agriculture worldwide is not practiced under these hotel conditions. Traditional African farmers do not aim for maximum yield because that, on the whole, is a fatuous thing to do. Much more important is to guarantee adequate yields in bad seasons – and in southern continents, beset not least by El Nino, bad seasons are frequent. More generally: yield cannot be maximized without huge capital investment, and the more you invest the more you are on the treadmill of debt, which alone has driven millions of farmers out of work. Applied to livestock, the single-minded maximization of yield is vile. Recent but still traditional dairy cows in Britain typically produced 600 to 800 gallons of milk per year for five years – and sometimes up to a decade or even more; whereas the modern cows, expected to average at least 1000 gallons and sometimes producing 2000 or more, average 1.8 lactations, after which they are crippled and have mastitis. In short: the maximization of yield, without proper regard to the circumstances, is ludicrous and sometimes foul. But it is what the modern economy demands.

The gratuitous adding of value is perhaps even more pernicious. Endless packaging and out-of-season vegetables whisked by jet from the far corners of the Earth are obviously gross. Less obvious, perhaps, but far more destructive – perhaps even the coup de grace – is the emphasis now placed on meat. For in truth from a commercial point of view it can be *too* easy to feed people well. People like the Turks who can make feasts out of cracked wheat do not need to spend a lot on food. So the grower has little scope for profit. The market is "inelastic". It has an obvious ceiling. That is bad news in an economy where growth is all.

The ceiling can be removed by adding value. Instead of selling wheat to people to turn into something great, feed it first to livestock. Animals consume anything from two-and-a-bit kg (in intensive poultry) up to about ten kg (in some cattle) of grain for every kg of meat they put on – and so the ceiling is removed both on production and on the sale-price of the product. The sudden surge in meat production in the West after World War II was justified at first by the idea that we need vast quantities of protein – but now this is known to be spurious. People do not need all that protein, and are positively laid low by too much saturated fat. In truth the driver has been commercial; adding value; removing the ceiling on production. So it is that nowadays, half of the world's wheat and about 80 per cent of the world's maize (plus well over 90 per cent of the soya and nearly all the barley that is not used for brewing) is fed to livestock. Of the major cereals, only rice is left more or less unscathed – people in rice-producing countries do indeed eat rice.

Livestock that feeds in places where crops cannot reasonably be grown, and on odds and ends, add to the human food supply. Those that are raised on staples that we could perfectly well be eating ourselves, compete with us. The United Nations calculates that by 2050, when the world population stands at nine billion, our livestock on the present rate of increase will be consuming the equivalent of another four billion. Four billion was roughly the population in the early 1970s when the United Nations held its first international conference to discuss what it saw as the pending food crisis. It would be relatively straightforward to feed nine billion – if we practised enlightened agriculture. Thirteen billion is another thing again. The increase in livestock in truth has very little indeed to do with human welfare. It has everything to do with the perceived need to maximize wealth.

Yet the third imperative of business – to minimize costs – is by far the worst of all. Firstly it is dangerous. The outbreaks of BSE, then foot and mouth disease (the largest epidemic ever), then swine fever, then foot and mouth again, and the recent, narrow squeaks with bird 'flu have all been brought about by cut-price husbandry. BSE happened because lactating cows were fed bits of dead cows as a cheap source of protein. This is aesthetically foul and is the antithesis of good practice – for proper farmers strive always to break chains of infection, but this created one where none existed before. The first and bigger foot and mouth outbreak happened through lack of surveillance and spread as rapidly as it did because so many abattoirs have been closed to save cash that animals are often sent across the country for the dubious privilege of being killed, spreading their pathogens as they go. Bird flu was brought in not by wild birds as was the original fear but on cut-price chickens imported from Hungary and Thailand. In truth, British livestock farming is now run on a wing and a prayer. Among other things, it is hugely irresponsible. But what the hell: it's cheap.

Worst of all though, is the effect on labour. In traditional systems, labour is the most expensive input. Therefore it has to be done away with. In Britain and the US only one per cent of the labour force works full time on the land. In the US more people are in jail than are on the land. Both claim that this is wonderfully "efficient" – and some economists in the US think that the exchange of farmers for prisoners is an advance (perhaps because prisons are such big business and contribute so handsomely to

GDP). In both countries this alleged "efficiency" is a fake because both supplement the legitimate labour force with immigrants of dubious legal status who are then allowed to slip through the net of human rights.

Foul though this is, however, the effects on the Third World are worse. In Third World countries, an average of 60% of the population live on the land. In India (where 60 per cent is indeed the figure) this is 600 million people – far bigger than the total population of the newly expanded European Union. Two hundred and fifty million of these are farmers – almost equaling the total population of the United States. Britain and the world's corporates have been urging the Third World as a whole to industrialize, like Britain and the US, in the name of "progress". But if they did then several billion people worldwide would be robbed of their livelihood. Unemployment is the royal road both to despair and to poverty – and while we perpetrate this nonsense, and drain away the Third World's cash in the form of "debt", we are running a fatuous, again fake, "war on poverty". I was told in India a few years ago that the farmers driven from the land could work in the new "alternative industries" — but this truly is unrealistic. IT was one of the industries cited – but IT employs tens of thousands; not hundreds of millions, as farming does. Tourism was mentioned too – but the same applies; and besides, the usual jobs in tourism (cleaning hotels before the tourists get up, and driving taxis for £8 a month) are no kind of improvement on farming, even when the farming is hard. Thus absurdity is piled on absurdity – all in the name of the modern economy.

In truth, the world cannot afford simply to industrialize. The industrialization of the west was a one-off. The only realistic future for most of the world is to remain agrarian – and countries like Britain and the US, way out on a precarious limb, should themselves become more agrarian rather than less with all possible speed. If 20 per cent of Britain's labour force worked on the land, that would hardly be too many. Of course, as things are, agrarian living can be ludicrously hard – but that is because farmers and farming are undervalued everywhere, and the overall economy, in the world as a whole, and in individual countries, in general is unsympathetic to the point of hostile: except, of course, for the huge grants handed out for industrialization, of which the farmers (agribusiness people) who are already rich get the lion's share.

In short, the modern economy is systematically killing off the kind of farming that could feed the world, and so it is systematically killing us. This is indictment enough.

Chapter 5

Where do we go from here?

So now to the heart of the matter. What kinds of economic institutions and mechanisms can provide us with the framework we need to do the kinds of things that we want to do and should be done within the physical limits of the real world? What form of *governance* can ensure that we finish up doing the things that so obviously need doing, and can produce the kind of world we want?

Governance

People at large – including governments – seem to take it for granted that government is necessary; and, indeed, that government should take roughly the form that it does in Britain or the US. Since both of those governments talk a great deal about democracy, and the need to defend democracy at all costs (even, apparently, at the expense of our personal freedoms), and since the political leaders in these countries are indeed elected, we tend to assume that democracy is what we have. Indeed, the idea is put about (and apparently is widely believed in Britain and the US) that our forms of government are about as good as it can get, and are a model for the whole world.

Yet a great many polls, and everyday experience, suggest that very few people in Britain or the US are satisfied with what their governments achieve. In both countries, too, the ruling party received only about a quarter of the available votes, yet seems to rule without serious opposition. Many therefore question the common conceit that what we have is true democracy. When we look at the world as a whole we rarely find government policies that are truly facing up to its deficiencies. Often, indeed, the strategies and policies of governments are at the root of the problem. Both in the US and in Britain, too, successive governments this past 30 years in particular have systematically ceded power to big business, in the form of corporates; the very opposite of what Thomas Jefferson perceived as the proper task of government, in the earliest days of the US. In short, in Britain and the US, we have governments that have more or less given up governing, in any worthwhile sense of the word. Yet they have enormous and apparently increasing power to interfere in all our lives, and so they do.

It is time to ask, as philosophers of politics have been asking for many thousands of years – most famously, in recent years, England's Thomas Hobbes – what it is that we want government to do; and indeed, while we are at it (since no stone should be left unturned) whether we need government at all.

A basic core of themes emerged in discussion after discussion in the Schumacher think-tank; not all pulling in quite the same direction, but adding up nonetheless to a potential sea-change. First, it is obvious that many people in the community at large have a far better grasp of what is good, and is worth doing, than is generally apparent in government. From this alone we can see the need and potential for grass-roots movements. Agriculture must be taken seriously – not just "a business like any other" but expressly designed to feed people, and re-built from the bottom up, using the skills and knowledge of the farmers – the people who actually do it for a living. The same principle applies to energy, and it is clearly implicit in the growing idea of local currencies. In education, too: one working group with Cherian Eapen, Brian Goodwin of Schumacher, Manfred Max-Neef of the Southern University in Chile, and Arturo Escobar of the University of North Carolina concluded that central governments should ensure that all schools even or especially in the poorest areas are well-endowed – but there their responsibility should end. To a very significant extent at least local people and indeed the teachers should decide what is actually taught. It is not the job of central government to impose a curriculum in minute detail, as has become the custom in England; and indeed it is very dangerous for them to do this, not least because of their shortness of vision. "Modern" education at all levels is increasingly geared to the status quo, which at least in principle makes it less and less easy to change direction.

On the other hand – as with Tariq's plan for an all-out global initiative to de-carbonize the South – we also need government at the highest level, above the national. Thus a working group convened by Satish Kumar agreed as a working rule that in general, 70 per cent of the economy should be local; 10 to 15 per cent regional; 5 per cent international; and only 10 per cent national. So they saw the power-structure as a pyramid, resting on a broad base of local government. Others, however, discussed a more dynamic approach – for example questioning the sanctity of "national". Apart from the odd island, national boundaries are historical accidents. They rarely make biogeographical, ethnic, or cultural sense. To design agriculture sensibly and sustainably we must think in terms of bioregion. Tariq Banuri wondered whether, in considering what forms of governance might serve us best, we should explore examples from biology. My glib answer is, "Of course we should". The human body is a master-class in cooperation, as trillions of potentially autonomous or quasi-autonomous cells, each with its consortium of 30,000 genes, conspire to create an entity so unified that it presumes to call itself "I". Controls are at all levels, from "master" glands such as the pituitary, down to the individual enzymes that edit DNA – two-way controls that are largely self-correcting and are entirely interdependent.

In short, we have lumbered ourselves with forms of government that no longer serve our best interests – and indeed, increasingly, seem hardly to be on our side. All kinds of forces keep those governments in place, including inertia and our own timidity – including our own fear of each other; apparently buying the idea we need some ruling body, armed to the teeth, to save us all from each other's treachery. In truth, we need to think radically about everything; and the role and nature of government, and the possible alternatives, must be very high on the agenda. This, too, is urgent. If we simply wait for governments to act on global warming, for example, then we will all be drowned before the relevant treaties have even got to the lawyers.

So what's to be done?

Renaissance and democracy

In principle, there are three ways to change society — and in the long run, to change the world.

The first is by Reform. People who want to change things talk to various factions within the society and try to edge them towards something different, and better. In practice, this is the route tried most often. Up to a point, it works. For instance, we have little hope of installing a radically different food system until and unless we have a food culture – until people at large, in their role as consumers, express serious dissatisfaction with the status quo and recognize what good food should look like. But reforms alone can never achieve what is now needed. For one thing, in these desperate times, it is too slow. More to the point, reform implies incremental change, step by step, from where we are to where we want to be. It is very difficult to see how, for example, transnational food companies that are expressly designed to scour the world for bargains could embrace systems of agriculture based on local production, labour-intensiveness, and fair dealings for all. If they did adopt such principles for anything more far-reaching than public relations, they would undermine their own raison d'etre. They would not generate the wealth that would satisfy their shareholders, and they would not do the job that really needs doing better than it could be done by other means. They would at best be superfluous to requirements.

The second route to change is by Revolution. This implies sweeping the board clean and starting again. Revolution has many drawbacks – there is even less chance than is usual in politics of staying in control of events, and achieving what was intended; it causes enormous collateral damage, which at the present time of history the world simply cannot afford. Besides, revolution is not going to happen. Even more to the point, revolution in the manner and on the scale achieved in Russia and China in the 20th century is not appropriate. We do not need to trash the present economy and begin from scratch. The radical economic notions proposed at the Schumacher meeting build upon the present-day fiscal mechanisms. They do no extirpate them to the roots.

The third is by the route already suggested: Renaissance. Don't try to change the status quo. Don't directly attack it. Don't pick fights we don't need to pick. Simply gather together a critical mass of people who know what they are doing, and give a damn, and start doing things differently. Begin locally, and regionally, and over time encourage the separate enterprises to coalesce.

Plenty of local and regional enterprises are afoot – in the offing, or already up and running – including the plethora of local and regional currencies and the Escos. Crucial, too, are the issues raised by Peter Barnes, of the Tomales Bay Institute, California, and a workshop with Juliet Schor of Boston College, Massachusetts, Frances Moore Lappé, and Arturo Escobar, of the University of North Carolina: different ways of controlling common land; different forms of ownership and entitlement. Again, the kinds of models that now seem to prevail, which often seem simply to give carte blanche to landowners to do as they will and increasingly treat land simply as another component of the portfolio, seem grotesque in a crowded world. But again, plenty of better models are already out there; even now, global corporate capitalism is not all there is. In Northern Italy, networks of 5000 small worker cooperatives produce nearly 40 per cent of the GDP (and, presumably, an at least commensurate slice of happiness). In general, so Juliet Schor's workshop concluded, we must "expand the range of experiences that can be considered credible alternatives to what exist". My own proposed Trust for Enlightened Agriculture is still notional but with luck will soon be providing such an alternative.

So the overall task, it seems, is two-fold. On the one hand we need seriously to redeploy government – away from mere nation states, up to the international level and down to the regional and local level. But we also need to transcend geographical boundaries and unite people of common interest wherever they are. Then we will have both the warp and woof of a truly democratic fabric that could itself be the stuff of governance – democratic by definition since it would grow from people's own initiatives.

Of course there have been many trans-geographical people's movements in the past – many kinds of clubs and trusts – which clearly have not achieved the kinds of global changes that are needed, so why should these emergent kinds be different? Partly because their scope is being extended to embrace areas that hitherto have been assumed to be the exclusive domain of government – notably the currency itself. Partly because more and more people are aware that conventional governance is failing us, and we need to re-think from first principles how we run our lives. Crucial, too, are new technologies that enable democracy to happen. This Schumacher think-tank was inspired both by Gandhi and by E. F. Schumacher. Both spoke of "appropriate technology"; Schumacher didn't simply say that "small is beautiful". Crucial, too, is the Austrian cultural historian Ivan Illich who in the 1960s wrote of "tools for conviviality" – technologies that increase human autonomy, as opposed to those that favour top-down control. Now we have the internet, and that may prove to be the most convivial of all: the technology that finally allows everyone to communicate easily and instantly with everyone else. Popular movements have rarely got far or made much impact because it has been so difficult for like-thinking people, however moral or smart, to cohere, and so to form a critical mass that can endure. The internet makes this possible.

It is as significant as writing or printing; truly, an evolutionary step. There are signs, worldwide, that people at large are beginning to feel their own power.

For the delegates at the Schumacher think-tank, November 2007 was not a one-off. All who took part perceive it as the start of something new that must persist — and has the collective influence to make a difference. Chile was mooted as the next grand meeting place but everyone will be active in the mean time and all are in dialogue with the rest. For practical purposes the group has now divided into "Flashpoints", producing solutions to immediate crises, and "Pole Star", thinking of the long-term future. These groups will communicate with the world at large, not least through the United Nations. This essay is only a preface, and a personal one at that, to the serious initiatives that will follow. In the past few years the hurricanes and floods have become too frequent to ignore, crops have been failing, and so many cracks have so obviously appeared in the neoliberal global agenda, that everyone now is taking an interest in the world's affairs. This is unprecedented; and it is what matters most of all.

SCHUMACHER COLLEGE THINK TANK
November 14 to 18, 2007
List of Participants

Tariq Banuri, Senior Fellow and Director of the Future Sustainability Program of the Stockholm Environment Institute,Tufts University, USA.

Peter Barnes, Senior Fellow at the Tomales Bay Institute, USA. Author of *Who Owns the Sky* and *Capitalism 3.0.*

Karen Blincoe, Director, Schumacher College.

Richard Douthwaite, Co-Founder of FEASTA (Foundation for the Economics of Sustainability), Ireland. Author of *The Growth Illusion* and *Short Circuit.*

Cherian Eapen, Founder of RIC Foundation, USA.

Paul Ekins, Professor of Energy and Environment Policy at King's College, London.

Arturo Escobar, Professor, Dept of Anthropology, University of North Carolina, USA. Author of *Encountering Development: The Making and Unmaking of the Third World.*

Brian Goodwin, Resident Scholar, Schumacher College.

Colin Hines, author of *Localization: A Global Manifesto*, advisor to Green MEP Caroline Lucas, Associate of International Forum on Globalisation.

Nadia Johanisova, teaches New Economics at Masaryk University, Czech Republic. Author of *Living in the Cracks: A Look at Rural Social Enterprises in Britain and the Czech Republic.*

Margrit Kennedy, MonNetA, Germany. Architect, consultant on complementary currencies and author of *Interest and Inflation-Free Money, Creating an Exchange Medium that works for Everybody and Protects the Earth.*

Miriam Kennet, Co-Founder and Director of Green Economics Institute, UK, Founder and Editor of International Journal of Green Economics and co-author of *Green Economics: Beyond Supply and Demand to Meeting People's Needs*

Satish Kumar, Programme Director, Schumacher College and Editor of *Resurgence* magazine.

Bernard Lietaer, Research Fellow at Center for Sustainable Resources, UC Berkeley, and Visiting Professor at Naropa University, USA. Author of *The Future of Money.*

Manfred Max-Neef, Southern University of Chile. Author of *From the Outside Looking In* and *Human-Scale Development.*

Frances Moore Lappé, Founder of Small Planet Institute, USA. Author of *Diet for a Small Planet* and *Democracy's Edge.*

Ann Pettifor, Executive Director of Advocacy International, UK and Co-Founder of Jubilee 2000. Author of *The Coming First World Debt Crisis.*

Julie Richardson, Director, Landscope, Dartington, UK.

Wolfgang Sachs, Fellow of Wuppertal Institute for Climate, Energy & the Environment, Germany. Author of the *Development Dictionary* and *Fair Future.*

Juliet Schor, Professor of Sociology at Boston College, USA and Co-Founder of Center for a New American Dream. Author of *Born to Buy, The Overspent American* and *The Overworked American.*

Vandana Shiva, Director of the Research Foundation for Science, Technology and Natural Resource Policy and Founder of Navdanya, India. Author of *Biopiracy, Stolen Harvest* and *Earth Democracy.*

Andrew Simms, Policy Director and head of Climate Change programme at nef (The New Economics Foundation). Author of *Ecological Debt* and *Tescopoly.*

Sulak Sivaraksa, Founder and Director of Spirit in Education Movement, and Founder of the International Network of Engaged Buddhists, Wongsanit Ashram and Santi Prachadhamma Institute, Thailand.

Colin Tudge, UK, scientist and author of *The Secret Life of Trees* and *Feeding People is Easy.*

Antony Turner, Founder and Director of CarbonSense, UK.

Facilitator: **James Martin-Jones** james@jamesmartinjones.com